Jumpstarters for Capitalization & Punctuation

Short Daily Warm-ups for the Classroom

By
CINDY BARDEN

COPYRIGHT © 2007 Mark Twain Media, Inc.

ISBN 978-1-58037-431-6

Printing No. CD-404078

Mark Twain Media, Inc., Publishers
Distributed by Carson-Dellosa Publishing Company, Inc.

Table of Contents

Introduction to the Teacher

Physical warm-ups help athletes prepare for more strenuous types of activity. Mental warm-ups help students prepare for the day's lesson while reviewing what they have previously learned.

The short warm-up activities presented in this book provide teachers and parents with activities to help students practice the skills they have already learned. Each page contains five warm-ups—one for each day of the week. Used at the beginning of class, warm-ups help students focus on a grammar-related topic.

The warm-up activities in this book cover punctuation skills including end-of-sentence punctuation, use of commas, apostrophes, colons, semicolons, dashes, quotation marks, contractions, and abbreviations. Capitalization skills include proper nouns and important words in specific names and titles of people, places, things, and animals. Students also practice sentence writing, rewriting proverbs, solving puzzles, writing headlines, and proofreading text.

Suggestions for use:

- Copy and cut apart one page each week. Give students one warm-up activity each day at the beginning of class.

- Give each student a copy of the entire page to complete day by day. Students can keep the completed pages in a three-ring binder to use as a resource.

- Make transparencies of individual warm-ups and complete the activities as a group.

- Provide extra copies of warm-ups in your learning center for students to complete at random when they have a few extra minutes.

- Keep some warm-ups on hand to use as fill-ins when the class has a few extra minutes before lunch or dismissal.

Punctuation Warm-ups:
Periods, Question Marks, & Exclamation Points

Name/Date _____

Periods, Question Marks, & Exclamation Points 1

Add punctuation at the end of each sentence.

1. How many chickens crossed the road

2. Look out for that hole

3. Does anyone know where the chickens went

4. Come quickly

5. Please put the feathers in the blue bag

6. Someone should fill in that hole

Name/Date _____

Periods, Question Marks, & Exclamation Points 2

On your own paper, write three sentences that end in exclamation points.

Name/Date _____

Periods, Question Marks, & Exclamation Points 3

On your own paper, write three sentences that end in question marks.

Name/Date _____

Periods, Question Marks, & Exclamation Points 4

On your own paper, rewrite the questions as declarative sentences.

1. Does Nicole have a brother?

2. Do you think Jon will be ready by noon?

3. Can Tammy win the race?

Name/Date _____

Periods, Question Marks, & Exclamation Points 5

On your own paper, write three sentences about your favorite sport or hobby. Use the correct end-of-sentence punctuation.

week 1

Punctuation Warm-ups: Periods, Questions Marks, & Exclamation Points

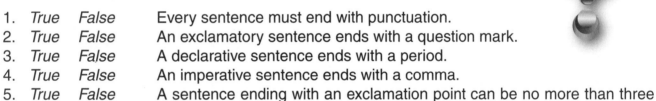

Name/Date _____

Periods, Question Marks, & Exclamation Points 6

Write the abbreviations, using a period.

1. Street   _____
2. Avenue   _____
3. Mister   _____
4. Senior   _____
5. Saint   _____
6. inch   _____
7. Junior   _____
8. Mountain   _____

COCONUT DRIVE

Name/Date _____

Periods, Question Marks, & Exclamation Points 7

Add periods after the initials in a person's name. Rewrite the names correctly.

1. J R R Tolkien _____
2. M T Lincoln _____
3. Mr P T Barnum _____
4. Mrs J C Parks _____
5. Dr M L King, Jr _____

Name/Date _____

Periods, Question Marks, & Exclamation Points 8

Circle *True* or *False*.

1. *True* *False*   Every sentence must end with punctuation.
2. *True* *False*   An exclamatory sentence ends with a question mark.
3. *True* *False*   A declarative sentence ends with a period.
4. *True* *False*   An imperative sentence ends with a comma.
5. *True* *False*   A sentence ending with an exclamation point can be no more than three words long.
6. *True* *False*   If a declarative or imperative sentence ends with an abbreviation, do not add a second period.

week 2

Name/Date _____

Periods, Question Marks, & Exclamation Points 9

Circle *Yes* or *No* to indicate if a period should be added at the end of the sentence.

1. *Yes* *No*   Rose Blvd. is near our school
2. *Yes* *No*   Max lives on Rose Blvd.
3. *Yes* *No*   Dr. Lee is a vet, not an M.D.
4. *Yes* *No*   Does Dr. Lee have a dentist appointment today
5. *Yes* *No*   I'll meet you at the YMCA

Name/Date _____

Periods, Question Marks, & Exclamation Points 10

Punctuate the sentences.

Oh Look at the shooting stars Do you think one will land nearby Have you ever seen so many shooting stars in one night What a wonderful experience I wonder if I will ever see a sight like this again Dr Young, the astronomer, said this is a very rare event

---

Punctuation Warm-ups: Commas

Name/Date _____

Commas 1

Add commas to separate the names of the cities from the states or countries.

1. Boise Idaho
2. Paris France
3. Taos New Mexico
4. Moscow Russia
5. Perth Australia

Name/Date _____

Commas 2

Write your birth date. _____
Write today's date. _____
When did you begin first grade? Write the month and year.

_____

What will the date be two months from today?

_____

Name/Date _____

Commas 3

Add commas to separate three or more words in a series.

1. How do oats peas beans and barley grow?
2. Please pick up bread milk potatoes carrots and apples at the store.
3. Would you like macaroni and cheese or a bacon lettuce and tomato sandwich for lunch?
4. Do you prefer baseball football golf hockey or tennis?

Name/Date _____

Commas 4

Finish the sentences on your own paper with a list of three words, using commas where needed.

At the mall, Amy bought…

At the zoo, we saw…

Tony said his best friends were…

My favorite subjects in school are…

Name/Date _____

_____

Commas 5

Add commas to separate a date from a year, but not a month.

Examples:
– *February 14, 2009* (add comma after 14)
– *February 2009* (no comma needed)

1. July 4 1776
2. February 1732
3. April 1885
4. September 1359
5. April 1 1963
6. August 31 1996
7. January 1 2000
8. December 15 1948

week 3

4

Punctuation Warm-ups:
Commas

Name/Date _____

Commas 6

Add commas to set off words not part of the quotations by Mark Twain.

1. "It is better to deserve honors" wrote Mark Twain "and not have them than to have them and not to deserve them."
2. "Let us so live that when we come to die even the undertaker will be sorry" he said.
3. "My mother had a great deal of trouble with me" Twain admitted "but I think she enjoyed it."
4. "Never put off until tomorrow what you can do the day after tomorrow" wrote Twain.
5. He also wrote "It is better to keep your mouth closed and let people think you are a fool than to open it and remove all doubt."

Name/Date _____

Commas 7

Write the names of six cities and states or cities and countries that you would like to visit.

_____
_____
_____
_____
_____
_____

Name/Date _____

Commas 8

Appositives are words that provide more information about a previous noun. Use commas to separate them from the rest of the sentence.
Example: Robert, whom we call Bob, called.

1. Abby the girl with the red scarf left.
2. Tell Glen who has freckles that Abby left.
3. Abby the girl who left is Glen's cousin.
4. Glen the quarterback broke his ankle.
5. Abby Glen's cousin is going to the game.

week 4

Name/Date _____

Commas 9

Write three sentences on your own paper using commas to separate appositives from the rest of the sentence.

Name/Date _____

Commas 10

Add commas after the introductory phrases.

1. Since you left the phone rang nine times.
2. When we cook the neighbors complain about the garlic smell.
3. Before you leave the dog should be fed.
4. If Grandma bakes her grandchildren will be delighted.
5. When it rains cats and dogs get wet.

Punctuation Warm-ups: Commas

Name/Date _____

Commas 11

On your own paper, write three sentences that begin with introductory phrases. Use commas and end-of-sentence punctuation correctly.

Name/Date _____

Commas 12

Add commas to set off nouns or pronouns in direct address from the rest of the sentence.

Examples: Tom, it's your job to paint the fence.
                       You can help too, Huck.

1.   Abby your mother called.
2.   Your mother called Abby
3.   Glen tell Abby her mother called.
4.   Did you listen Abby to what Glen said?
5.   I can't find Abby Glen.

Name/Date _____

Commas 13

On your own paper, write three sentences using commas to set off nouns in direct address.

"Jed, will you ..."

Name/Date _____

Commas 14

Add commas and end-of-sentence punctuation to Sara's letter.

Dear Aunt Sally

        Thank you for offering to bring dip chips and veggies for the cookout Our neighbors the Falks have a dog When we barbecue the dog barks Do you think I should buy dog treats Then while we eat the dog might be quiet for a while

                                        Your niece
                                        Sara

week 5

Name/Date _____

Commas 15

Add a comma after *yes* or *no* when it is the first word of a sentence.

1.   Yes we plan to meet Bret tomorrow after the game.
2.   I wanted to stay for the postgame party, but Bret said no.
3.   No I don't know if Bret said yes or no to the contract.
4.   Bret, did you decide to say yes to the contract?
5.   "Yes We Have No Bananas" is the name of an old song.

Punctuation Warm-ups: Commas

Name/Date _____

Commas 16

Add commas where needed.

SPEEDING TICKET
WHOA, PONY!
FINE: $5

1. When Abraham Lincoln was a lawyer he carried important papers in his top hat.
2. Before he became president Ulysses S. Grant was arrested twice for speeding.
3. For riding his horse too fast he was fined $5.
4. George Washington Thomas Jefferson and John Adams enjoyed collecting and playing marbles even as adults.

Name/Date _____

Commas 17

Add commas where needed.

1. John Quincy Adams sixth president of the United States planted mulberry trees on the White House lawn.
2. His wife Louisa spun silk from silkworms.
3. To relax Adams liked to go for walks play pool and swim in the Potomac River.
4. Born in a log cabin Millard Fillmore didn't attend school until he was 19 years old.

Name/Date _____

Commas 18

Add commas where needed.

On December 17 1903 Orville and Wilbur Wright made the first successful flight in a heavier-than-air machine. Their airplane didn't fly very far (only about 120 feet) very fast (only 30 mph) very high (only a few feet off the ground) or very long (only 12 seconds) but it did fly.

Name/Date _____

Commas 19

Add commas where needed.

In 1938 Douglas Corrigan an unemployed airplane mechanic left Brooklyn New York to fly to Los Angeles California. When he landed 28 hours and 13 minutes later he found himself in Dublin Ireland. Because he claimed he had accidentally followed the wrong end of the compass needle he received the nickname "Wrong Way" Corrigan.

Week 6

Name/Date _____

Commas 20

Match the ways to use commas with the examples.

1. _____ After an introductory phrase
2. _____ After the greeting in a friendly letter
3. _____ After the closing in a letter
4. _____ To set off words in direct address
5. _____ To separate appositives
6. _____ Between the day and the year
7. _____ Between cities and states
8. _____ To separate nouns in a series

A. April 14, 1775
B. I'd like a cheese, tuna, and onion pizza.
C. Tim, Mary's son, is the team's star pitcher.
D. When the moon rose, the wolves howled.
E. Yours truly,
F. Las Vegas, Nevada
G. Dear Sherlock Holmes,
H. Mr. Watson, come here please.

7

Punctuation Warm-ups:
Commas

Name/Date _____

Commas 21

Circle *Yes* if the commas are used correctly or *No* if not.

1. *Yes No* May 6, 1927
2. *Yes No* May, 1927
3. *Yes No* Rio de Janeiro, Brazil
4. *Yes No* New Orleans Louisiana,
5. *Yes No* Easter, Sunday
6. *Yes No* Jan grew peas beans corn tomatoes and peppers in her garden.

Name/Date _____

Commas 22

On your own paper, write an introductory phrase to complete each sentence. Set it off with a comma.

1. …we found our way.
2. …then she said good-bye.
3. …but no one listened to me.
4. …then Ian knew he had found his destiny.
5. …the baby will be fine.

Name/Date _____

Commas 23

Write appositives to complete the sentences. Use commas correctly.

1. Mary _____ grew silver bells and cockleshells.

2. Jack _____ jumped over the candlestick.

3. Jack and Jill _____ fetched some water.

4. Humpty Dumpty _____ couldn't be mended.

5. Little Miss Muffet _____ ran away.

week 7

Name/Date _____

Commas 24

Write words in direct address to complete the sentences. Use commas correctly.

1. _____ would you like to go skiing next weekend?
2. Would you _____ like to go skiing?
3. Would you like to go skiing _____?
4. Sorry _____ I can't go skiing this weekend.

Name/Date _____

Commas 25

Fill in the blanks to complete the letter. Add commas where needed.

Dear _____

    I'm going to _____ Ohio next weekend. Rob _____ and _____ are planning to go along. Do you remember Rob _____ last year? We'll leave _____ Iowa at 5 A.M. Friday morning.

    Yours truly

    _____

8

Punctuation Warm-ups: Apostrophes to Show Possession

Name/Date _____

_____

Apostrophes to Show Possession 1

Rewrite each group of words to show possession.

Example: boys have dogs – the boys' dogs

1. the eggs of three hens

_____

2. the homes of two families

_____

3. the gardens of the women

_____

4. the honey of many bees

_____

5. the trees of the forests

_____

6. the desks of the teachers

_____

Name/Date _____

Apostrophes to Show Possession 2
Rewrite each group of words to show possession.
Example: a boy has a dog – the boy's dog

1. the song of a child   _____
2. the antlers of a deer   _____
3. the tail of the mouse   _____
4. the scent of a rose   _____
5. the capital of Italy   _____

Name/Date _____

Apostrophes to Show Possession 3
Rewrite the underlined noun to plural and to show possession.
Example: the children of the <u>woman</u> – the women's children

1. the wheels of the <u>bus</u>   _____
2. the laughter of the <u>child</u>   _____
3. the sounds of the <u>factory</u>   _____
4. the gardens of the <u>lady</u>   _____
5. the howls of the <u>wolf</u>   _____

Name/Date _____

Apostrophes to Show Possession 4
Rewrite the underlined noun to plural and to show possession.

1. the <u>tale</u> of the tiger   _____
2. the <u>growl</u> of the bear   _____
3. the <u>light</u> of the city   _____
4. the <u>child</u> of the man   _____
5. the <u>shoe</u> of the horse   _____
6. the <u>city</u> of Maine   _____

Name/Date _____

Apostrophes to Show Possession 5
Change both nouns to plural and rewrite to show possession.

1. the tooth of the shark   _____
2. the foot of the fox   _____
3. the berry on the bush   _____
4. the squeal of the mouse   _____
5. the scarf of the elf   _____

week 8

Punctuation Warm-ups: Apostrophes to Show Possession

Name/Date _____

Apostrophes to Show Possession 6

Write six phrases that show possession using singular nouns.

Example: the plant's stem

_____

_____

_____

_____

_____

_____

Name/Date _____

Apostrophes to Show Possession 7

Write six phrases that show possession using plural nouns.

Example: the flowers' petals

_____

_____

_____

_____

_____

_____

Name/Date _____

Apostrophes to Show Possession 8

Write the plural of the nouns shown. Add a singular possessive noun to show ownership.

Example: pony – Edward's ponies

1. leaf   _____
2. foot   _____
3. man   _____
4. cherry   _____
5. tooth   _____
6. animal   _____

week 9

Name/Date _____

Apostrophes to Show Possession 9

Write the plural of the noun shown. Add a plural possessive noun to show ownership.

Example: pony – the children's ponies

1. flower   _____
2. horse   _____
3. fireman   _____
4. goose   _____
5. fish   _____

Name/Date _____

Apostrophes to Show Possession 10

Write the plural possessive form of the noun. Add a singular noun to show what is owned.

Example: child – children's parent

1. group   _____
2. aunt   _____
3. monkey   _____
4. person   _____
5. puppy   _____
6. buddy   _____

Punctuation Warm-ups: Apostrophes to Show Possession

Name/Date _____

Apostrophes to Show Possession 11

Write the plural possessive form of the noun. Add a plural noun to show what is owned.

Example: child – children's parents

1. spy _____
2. moose _____
3. ox _____
4. piano _____
5. tomato _____
6. mosquito _____

Name/Date _____

Apostrophes to Show Possession 12

Is the apostrophe used correctly to show possession? Circle *Yes* or *No*

1. Yes No How was the children's recital?
2. Yes No How long is the phones' cord?
3. Yes No Hannah's' purse was heavy.
4. Yes No The storm damaged three families' cars.
5. Yes No Her's book was lost.
6. Yes No Did he find his' snake?

Name/Date _____

Apostrophes to Show Possession 13

Circle the error in each sentence. Rewrite the word correctly.

1. _____ That is it's home.
2. _____ Where are Sues's socks?
3. _____ Pick up the daisys petals.
4. _____ Is that you's comb?
5. _____ My grandmothers' ring was in her cedar chest.
6. _____ Both of my grandfather's came here from Ireland.

Name/Date _____

Apostrophes to Show Possession 14

On another sheet of paper, write a short paragraph about your school. Include at least five possessive nouns.

week 10

Name/Date _____

Apostrophes to Show Possession 15

Circle the two errors in each quotation. Rewrite the words correctly.

1. _____ A countryman between two lawyer's is like a fish between two cat's.
   _____ — Benjamin Franklin
2. _____ Human's are not proud of their ancestor's, and rarely invite them round
   _____ to dinner. — Douglas Adams
3. _____ Do not worry about your difficulties' in Mathematics'. I can assure you
   _____ mine are still greater. — Albert Einstein
4. _____ A nations treasure is in its scholars'. — Chinese Proverb
   _____

Punctuation Warm-ups: Apostrophes With Contractions

Name/Date _____

Apostrophes With Contractions 1

Rewrite each pair of words as a contraction.

1. I am   _____
2. you are   _____
3. he is   _____
4. she will   _____
5. is not   _____
6. it had   _____
7. they would   _____
8. we have   _____

Name/Date _____

Apostrophes With Contractions 2

Rewrite each pair of words as a contraction.

1. are not   _____
2. will not   _____
3. they will   _____
4. could have   _____
5. we are   _____
6. where is   _____
7. could not   _____
8. how is   _____

Name/Date _____

Apostrophes With Contractions 3

Circle the apostrophe errors. Rewrite the words correctly.

1. _____ You cant tell a book by its cover.
2. _____ Dont count your chickens before they hatch.
3. _____ Bird's of a feather flock together.
4. _____ Were all in the same boat.
5. _____ Hes trying to burn the candle at both ends.
6. _____ Its time to lay all the cards on the table.

Name/Date _____

Apostrophes With Contractions 4

Rewrite each pair of words as a contraction.

1. he would   _____
2. she had   _____
3. I will   _____
4. they are   _____
5. it is   _____
6. we were   _____
7. you have   _____
8. must not   _____

Name/Date _____

Apostrophes With Contractions 5

Circle the contraction errors. Rewrite the contractions correctly.

1. He isnt sorry. Those are crocodile tears. _____
2. I wont throw you a curve. _____
3. Were on the cutting edge of technology. _____
4. My teachers looking daggers at me. _____

Punctuation Warm-ups: Apostrophes With Contractions

Name/Date _____

Apostrophes With Contractions 6

Rewrite each pair of words as a contraction.

1. do not   _____
2. I would   _____
3. does not   _____
4. she is   _____
5. did not   _____
6. we would   _____
7. he had   _____
8. has not   _____

Name/Date _____

Apostrophes With Contractions 7

Rewrite each pair of words as a contraction.

1. they had   _____
2. he will   _____
3. cannot   _____
4. how had   _____
5. had not   _____
6. have not   _____
7. he has   _____
8. how would   _____

Name/Date _____

Apostrophes With Contractions 8

Circle the contraction errors.
Rewrite the contractions correctly.

1. It wont help to jump out of the frying pan into the fire. _____
2. Shes a loose cannon. _____
3. Thats the way the cookie crumbles. _____
4. Jamie didnt want to rock the boat. _____

Name/Date _____

Apostrophes With Contractions 9

Rewrite each pair of words as a contraction.

1. _____ I have
2. _____ how has
3. _____ I had
4. _____ must have
5. _____ might not
6. _____ should have
7. _____ we have
8. _____ were not

Name/Date _____

Apostrophes With Contractions 10

Circle the contraction errors in these quotations. Rewrite the contractions correctly.

1. _____ If opportunity doesnt knock, build a door. — Milton Berle
2. _____ Dont worry about the world coming to an end today.
   _____ Its already tomorrow in Australia.   — Charles M. Schulz
3. _____ I have a new philosophy. Im only going to dread one day at a time.
                                                               — Charles M. Schulz
4. _____ If only wed stop trying to be happy, we could have a pretty good time.
                                                               — Edith Wharton

---

Punctuation Warm-ups:
Apostrophes With Contractions

Name/Date _____

Apostrophes With Contractions 11

Rewrite each pair of words as a contraction.

1. _____ it would
2. _____ it will
3. _____ might have
4. _____ she would
5. _____ that will
6. _____ we will
7. _____ they would
8. _____ who will

Name/Date _____

Apostrophes With Contractions 12

Rewrite each pair of words as a contraction.

1. _____ it has
2. _____ she has
3. _____ should not
4. _____ that had
5. _____ they have
6. _____ was not
7. _____ we had
8. _____ who is

Name/Date _____

Apostrophes With Contractions 13

Circle the contraction errors. Rewrite the contractions correctly.

1. _____ There waiting for the dust to settle.

2. _____ Shell have to eat her words.

3. _____ It wouldnt hurt to apply a little elbow grease to the problem.

4. _____ Thats as difficult as an elephant trying to lay an egg.

5. _____ Your acting like a large frog in a small pond.

Name/Date _____

Apostrophes With Contractions 14

Rewrite each pair of words as a contraction.

1. _____ that is
2. _____ when will
3. _____ we will
4. _____ who would
5. _____ would have
6. _____ you have
7. _____ would not
8. _____ you would

Name/Date _____

Apostrophes With Contractions 15

Rewrite each pair of words as a contraction.

1. _____ when is
2. _____ you will
3. _____ we would
4. _____ what are
5. _____ what will
6. _____ where will
7. _____ what is
8. _____ who has

14

Punctuation Warm-ups: Apostrophe Review

Name/Date _____

Apostrophe Review 1

Circle the correct words.

1. (It's/Its) time for (your/you're) dog's appointment with the vet.
2. My puppy likes to chase (it's/its) tail.
3. Does (your/you're) puppy do that too?
4. (Whose/Who's) dog is that?
5. "(Whose/Who's) next?" asked the vet.

Name/Date _____

Apostrophe Review 2

Circle the correct words.

1. (Whose/Who's) ready for the test?
2. The boy (whose/who's) father is a baker brought donuts for the class.
3. (There/Their/They're) planning to visit Spain next summer.
4. Sit (there/their/they're) while you wait.
5. Will you be going to (there/their/they're) party?

Name/Date _____

Apostrophe Review 3

Circle the correct words.

1. That camera is (there's/theirs).
2. (There's/Theirs) more than one way to study for a test.
3. "(There's/Theirs) no place like home, Toto," said Dorothy.
4. (Who's/Whose) ready for another adventure?
5. "(Your/You're) welcome," Beth said.

Name/Date _____

Apostrophe Review 4

Circle the correct words.

1. The five (boys'/boy's) bikes were outside.
2. (Greece's/Greeces) national anthem has 158 verses!
3. Have you read *The (Hitchhiker's/Hitchhikers) Guide to the Galaxy*?
4. "That's fine as (frog's/frogs) hair," Jess said.
5. Joe (Jackson's/Jacksons) nickname was "Shoeless Joe."

Name/Date _____

Apostrophe Review 5

Circle the correct words. Can you answer these riddles?

1. How long should a (giraffe's/giraffes) legs be? _____
2. What did (dinosaurs/dinosaur's) have that no other animals have ever had?

_____

3. What (animals/animal's) should carry an oil can?

_____

4. What is smaller than an (ant's/ants') mouth? _____
5. What's The Lone (Ranger's/Rangers) first name? _____

Punctuation Warm-ups: Quotation Marks

Name/Date _____

Quotation Marks 1

Use quotation marks and capitalize all the important words in titles of songs. Important words include the first word, all nouns, pronouns, verbs, adjectives, adverbs, and words that have five or more letters.

On your own paper, write the titles of six songs.

Example: "The Little Old Lady from Pasadena"

Name/Date _____

Quotation Marks 2

Use quotation marks and capitalize all the important words in titles of short stories. On your own paper, write the titles of four short stories.

Example: "The Ugly Duckling"

Name/Date _____

Quotation Marks 3

Rewrite the titles of these articles from newspapers, magazines, and encyclopedias. Use quotation marks and capitalize the important words.

1. ox cart drag racing _____

2. football stars from the past _____

3. 7 ways to become a millionaire _____

4. the best artichoke recipes _____

5. dog with college degree called to court

_____

Name/Date _____

Quotation Marks 4

Use quotation marks and capitalize important words in names of TV shows. On your own paper, write the names of four TV shows.

Example: "Jeopardy"

Name/Date _____

Quotation Marks 5

Use quotation marks and capitalize important words in titles of poems. On your own paper, write the titles of six nursery rhymes or other poems.

Example: "Who Has Seen the Wind?"

Punctuation Warm-ups:
Quotation Marks

Name/Date _____

Quotation Marks 6

Add quotation marks.

1. O Captain! My Captain! is a famous poem about Abraham Lincoln by Walt Whitman.
2. The television show Gunsmoke was on the air for 20 years.
3. Many people continue to enjoy watching re-runs of Star Trek.
4. Did you read the article Girl Calls 911: Grandpa Cheats at Cards today?

Name/Date _____

Quotation Marks 7

Add quotation marks to set off the exact words of a speaker. Add end-of-sentence punctuation inside the final quotation marks.

Example: "Where are you going?" he asked.

1. Sara shouted, Look out
2. Are we there yet Tina asked
3. Tammy answered, We'll be there soon
4. But when Tina whined
5. Where did you come from Troy asked

Name/Date _____

Quotation Marks 8

Add commas, quotation marks, and end-of-sentence punctuation. Use the example as a guideline.

Example: "I understand," she said, "and will try to help if I can."

1. Suddenly said Caesar I understand what you mean
2. I may not have gone where I intended to go wrote Douglas Adams but I think I have ended up where I needed to be

3. It is a mistake the author of *The Hitchhiker's Guide to the Galaxy* wrote to think you can solve any major problems just with potatoes
4. Please buy some eggs George told his son and also a gallon of milk

---

Name/Date _____

Quotation Marks 9

Finish the sentences.

1. "_____?" asked Jerry
2. "Well," said Linda, "I think _____ _____."
3. "I agree," Jerry said, "but _____ _____."
4. "Then we could _____ _____," agreed Linda.

Name/Date _____

Quotation Marks 10

Finish the sentences. Add punctuation where needed.

1. What _____ _____ asked the waitress
2. I'll have _____ _____ said Karen
3. Would you like _____ _____ she asked.
4. I'll have _____ _____ instead said Karen

Punctuation Warm-ups: Colons & Semicolons

Name/Date _____

Colons & Semicolons 1

Add semicolons between closely related independent clauses not joined by a conjunction (*and, or, nor, for, yet, but*).

Example: Adam wanted an orange; Eve wanted an apple.

1. Brian thought she was kind I thought she was grouchy.
2. "I came I saw I conquered," wrote Julius Caesar.
3. Jessica wrote short stories she also wrote poetry.
4. Pam needed a new coat her old one was too small.
5. The blizzard was bad the planes could not land.

Name/Date _____

Colons & Semicolons 2

Add colons after the salutation in a business letter, between the hour and the minute, and before a list of three or more items.

Dear Mayor

    After attending the 7 00 meeting last evening, I had three concerns the number of snowplows available, the training of personnel, and the plowing schedule for the school parking lots.

Name/Date _____

Colons & Semicolons 3

Add colons where needed.

Dear Mr. Jones

    I will arrive at 6 30 today to pick up the six items for my office we discussed the new computer, printer, monitor, scanner, telephone, and desk.

    Sincerely,
    Matt Pyatt

Name/Date _____

Colons & Semicolons 4

Add colons and semicolons where needed.

Dear Brenda,

    Please do these chores when you get home at 3 00 clean your room, start the laundry, and put the roast in the oven. I will see you at 5 45 your father will be home at 6 00.

    Mom

Name/Date _____

Colons & Semicolons 5

Write a short sentence on your own paper using each type of punctuation correctly.

Colon

Semicolon

Apostrophe

Comma

Punctuation Warm-ups: Punctuation Review

_____

Punctuation Review 1

Choose one of the sports listed below for each group of punctuation listed. Write a short sentence on your own paper for each one.

basketball	golf
football	baseball
volleyball	hockey

1. quotation marks and commas
2. semicolon and question mark
3. apostrophe and exclamation point
4. colon and period

Punctuation Review 2

1. The three types of end punctuation are _____, _____, and _____.
2. Use a _____ when asking a question.
3. An _____ shows surprise, fear, or strong feelings.
4. Use a _____ when giving a command.
5. Use a _____ when stating a fact.

Punctuation Review 3

Rewrite the sentences on your own paper, and add punctuation where needed.
1. Harry Potter the boy who lived is a fictional character
2. While Doris ate the mice waited for crumbs
3. After Jen finished sweeping the wind blew the dirt back
4. Until 1958 the Dodgers played in Brooklyn New York
5. Paul please wash dry and put away the dishes

Punctuation Review 4

Rewrite the paragraph on your own paper, and add punctuation where needed.

In 1885 Gottlieb Daimler a German inventor built the first motorcycle by attaching a small gasoline engine to a wooden bicycle frame The wooden wheels came from a horse-drawn carriage the seat was a leather horses saddle Early motorcycles had pedals like bikes The engines werent strong enough to go up hills so riders had to pedal

Punctuation Review 5

Rewrite the paragraph on your own paper, and add punctuation where needed.

The engines on early motorcycles werent very reliable Unfortunately they often broke down Riders carried gasoline with them because there were no gas stations Fortunately if the engine didnt work or the motorcycle ran out of gas the rider could always keep pedaling Can you imagine a group of Harley riders pedaling down the highway today

Punctuation Warm-ups:
Punctuation Review

Name/Date _____

Punctuation Review 6

Circle *Yes* or *No* to indicate if the sentence is punctuated correctly. If no, make corrections.

1. *Yes   No*   Henry Wadsworth Longfellows poem Paul Reveres Ride was very popular in the 1860s.
2. *Yes   No*   Longfellow wrote about a real event but he changed the facts a bit
3. *Yes   No*   Paul Revere became the hero of the poem.
4. *Yes   No*   Do you know what really happened?
5. *Yes   No*   On the night of April 18 1775 Paul Revere left Boston.
6. *Yes   No*   Revere rode to Lexington to warn Samuel Adams' and John Hancock that British soldiers planned to arrest them.

Name/Date _____

Punctuation Review 7

Circle *Yes* or *No* to indicate if the sentence is punctuated correctly. If no, make corrections.

1. *Yes   No*   Revere also needed to alert the patriots in nearby Concord about a British raid.
2. *Yes   No*   On his way to Lexington he stopped at houses to deliver a warning:
3. *Yes   No*   William Dawes also set out to deliver the same warnings but he took a different route.

Name/Date _____

Punctuation Review 8

Circle *Yes* or *No* to indicate if the sentence is punctuated correctly. If no, make corrections.

1. *Yes   No*   "The British are coming!" Revere shouted.
2. *Yes   No*   About midnight he gave Adams and Hancock the message they had time to escape.
3. *Yes   No*   When Dawes arrived, he and Paul Revere set off for Concord.

Name/Date _____

Punctuation Review 9

Circle *Yes* or *No* to indicate if the sentence is punctuated correctly. If no, make corrections.

1. *Yes   No*   On the way, Dr Samuel Prescott joined them.
2. *Yes   No*   Before they reached Concord, a British patrol arrested the men.
3. *Yes   No*   Dawes and Prescott escaped but Dawes fell off his horse.
4. *Yes   No*   Dawes couldn't continue.

Name/Date _____

Punctuation Review 10

Circle *Yes* or *No* to indicate if the sentence is punctuated correctly. If no, make corrections.

1. *Yes   No*   The British took away Paul Reveres horse.
2. *Yes   No*   He walked back to Lexington.
3. *Yes   No*   Prescott, reached Concord.
4. *Yes   No*   Prescotts early warning helped the patriot's win the first battle of the Revolutionary War.

20

Punctuation Warm-ups: Punctuation Review

Name/Date _____

Punctuation Review 11

On your own paper, list several ways that end-of-sentence punctuation helps us when reading an article or story.

Name/Date _____

Punctuation Review 12

What purposes do commas serve?

_____

_____

_____

_____

_____

Name/Date _____

Punctuation Review 13

In your opinion, what is the most important (useful) type of punctuation? Explain your reasons on another sheet of paper.

Name/Date _____

Punctuation Review 14

On your own paper, give two examples of sentences that would be confusing without punctuation and explain why.

Name/Date _____

Punctuation Review 15

Add punctuation where needed.

 Buffalo Bill Cody had little formal education When he wrote his life story the publisher complained about Codys punctuation and capitalization Life is too short to make big letters where small ones will do replied Cody And as for punctuation if my readers don't know enough to take their breath without those little marks they'll have to lose it that's all

Punctuation Warm-ups: Punctuation Review

Name/Date _____

_____

Punctuation Review 16

Unscramble the letters to form words related to punctuation.

1. iupnutnocat

_____

2. notaquoit samrk

_____

3. momac

_____

4. tosinueq krams

_____

5. malatecixon otinp

_____

6. loonsc

_____

7. scomelions

_____

8. potrospehas

_____

9. rediop

_____

Name/Date _____

Punctuation Review 17

Circle the phrase that is punctuated correctly.

1. Yours truly,   Yours truly;   Yours truly: Yours truly.
2. Dear Angie;   Dear Angie,   Dear Angie: Dear Angie.
3. May 1: 1902   May 1; 1902   May 1. 1902   May 1, 1902
4. 4,15 A.M.   4;15 A.M.   4:15 A.M.   4.15 A.M.
5. Rome, Italy   Rome; Italy   Rome: Italy   Rome. Italy

Name/Date _____

Punctuation Review 18

Make corrections to the sentences.
1. Pecos Bill, a cowboy, was a hero in many tall tales!
2. Sam have you ever wanted to be a superhero.
3. What would be a good name for a superhero hamster Herman?
4. Mighty Mouse, a cartoon character always arrived in the nick of time.

Name/Date _____

Punctuation Review 19

Make corrections to the sentences.
1. Spitting on your hand's before picking up the bat is good luck.
2. A wad of gum stuck on a players hat is good luck.
3. It is bad luck if a dog walk's across the diamond.
4. Lending a bat to a fellow player bring's bad luck.
5. Sleeping with your bat will help end a hitting slump?

Name/Date _____

Punctuation Review 20

Add punctuation to these proverbs.
1. A rolling stone gathers no moss
2. Every cloud has a silver lining
3. A stitch in time saves nine
4. A penny saved is a penny earned
5. You cant teach an old dog new tricks

Capitalization Warm-ups: Proper Nouns

Name/Date _____

Proper Nouns 1

Use correct capitalization to write the first and last names of five people you know.

_____

_____

_____

_____

_____

Name/Date _____

Proper Nouns 2

Use correct capitalization to write the names of three days of the week and three months of the year.

Days   Months

_____

_____

_____

Name/Date _____

Proper Nouns 3

Use correct capitalization to write the names of four holidays.

_____

_____

_____

_____

Name/Date _____

Proper Nouns 4

Use correct capitalization to write the names of three countries and the nouns derived from those countries' names.

Example: China; Chinese

_____

_____

_____

Name/Date _____

Proper Nouns 5

Circle the capitalization errors.

1. sunday, march 15, we will travel to mexico.
2. thanksgiving is celebrated on the fourth thursday in november.
3. For supper, Jason ordered a salad with french dressing, german chocolate cake, and italian spaghetti.
4. dolly madison, mary todd lincoln, abigail adams, and martha washington were famous first ladies.

Capitalization Warm-ups: Proper Nouns

Name/Date _____

Proper Nouns 6

Circle the capitalization errors in these weird facts.

1. In 1656, captain kemble of boston was sentenced to sit in the stocks for two hours because of improper behavior on a sunday.
2. he had kissed his Wife in public after returning from a three-year sea voyage!
3. a dog was convicted of killing a Cat and sent to prison in 1925.
4. He died of Old Age after spending his last six years in a prison in philadelphia.
5. In 1939, pinball machines were illegal in atlanta, georgia.
6. In 1660, massachusetts outlawed the celebration of christmas.
7. offenders were fined Five shillings.

Name/Date _____

Proper Nouns 7

Circle the capitalization errors.

1. in philadelphia, pennsylvania, in 1912, 15 women lost their jobs at the curtis publishing company for dancing at work.
2. in 1674, 30 men were arrested in connecticut for wearing silk and having long hair.
3. In 1712, people who drove their Wagons recklessly in philadelphia were fined for speeding.

Name/Date _____

Proper Nouns 8

Circle the capitalization errors.

1. Electricity was installed in the white house while benjamin harrison was President.
2. Harrison and his Wife feared it; they refused to touch any of the switches.
3. sometimes they left the lights on all night if Servants weren't available to turn them off.
4. president jackson had little formal education as a child.

Name/Date _____

Proper Nouns 9

Circle the capitalization errors.

1. Honey discovered in the tombs of egyptian pharaohs is still edible.
2. Egyptians believed that the creator god, khnum, made each person on his potter's wheel.
3. The greek historian herodotus reported that when a family's pet Cat died, egyptians mourned the loss by shaving off their eyebrows.

Name/Date _____

Proper Nouns 10

Circle the capitalization errors.

1. The ancient egyptians had a taxation and legal system with a Police force and courts.
2. One way to pay Taxes was to send Servants to work part of the year for the Pharaoh.
3. Beating was the most common form of punishment for Criminals and those who did not pay their Taxes.

Capitalization Warm-ups:
Proper Nouns

Name/Date _____

Proper Nouns 11

Why do you think it's important to capitalize the first word of each sentence? Write your response on your own paper.

Name/Date _____

Proper Nouns 12

Write the names of three U.S. and three international cities.

_____

_____

_____

_____

_____

_____

Name/Date _____

Proper Nouns 13

Capitalize the names of pets. Write a good name for each type of pet.

1. a hamster _____

2. a snake _____

3. a skunk _____

4. a horse _____

5. a parrot _____

6. a goldfish _____

7. a hedgehog _____

8. a tarantula _____

Name/Date _____

Proper Nouns 14

1. What month is it?_____

2. What is today?_____

4. What was yesterday?_____

5. What was the last holiday?

_____

6. What will the next holiday be?

_____

Name/Date _____

Proper Nouns 15

If the words in parentheses are not capitalized correctly, make corrections.

(George) (samuelson) and (frank) (Harbo) crossed the (atlantic) (Ocean) in 1894. (they) left (new) (York) on (june) 6 and landed in (England) on (august) 1, 1894. (george) and (Frank) weren't the first to make the perilous (journey) across the (Ocean), but they did it the hard way—in a (Rowboat)!

25

Capitalization Warm-ups: Important Words

Name/Date _____

Important Words 1

Capitalize the important words in people's names.

1. king henry of england _____
2. emperor julius casear _____
3. queen isabella of spain _____
4. president gerald r. ford _____
5. lawrence of arabia _____

Name/Date _____

Important Words 2

Capitalize the important words in the names of places.

1. the grand canyon _____
2. the golden gate bridge _____
3. st. louis gateway arch _____
4. the pyramids of giza _____
5. mount st. helens _____

Name/Date _____

Important Words 3

Write an example for each item listed. Use capitalization.

1. a mountain _____
2. a canyon _____
3. a river _____
4. a lake _____
5. a volcano _____

Name/Date _____

Important Words 4

Capitalize important words in specific names.

1. the constitution _____
2. the statue of liberty _____
3. the great wall of china _____
4. the taj mahal _____
5. the gettysburg address _____

Name/Date _____

_____

Important Words 5

Circle the 10 capitalization errors in this paragraph.

The statue of zeus at olympia was one of the seven wonders of the ancient world. This 40-foot-tall seated figure of zeus, king of the greek gods, was carved in the mid-5th century B.C. by phidias. It was the central feature of the temple of zeus at olympia, home to the ancient olympic games in greece.

Capitalization Warm-ups: Important Words

Name/Date _____

Important Words 6

Circle the 15 capitalization errors. Rewrite the words correctly on another sheet of paper.

1. In 1970, a 1.67 pound hailstone fell in coffeyville, texas.
2. An Earthquake in missouri on november 16, 1811, caused the missis-sippi river to flow backwards
3. george washington had two ice-cream freezers at his home in mount vernon.
4. Mother Nature dumped 189 inches of snow on mount shasta, california, during a storm that lasted from february 13 to 19, 1959.

Name/Date _____

Important Words 7

Capitalize the important words in the names of these fictional animals.

1. bugs bunny _____
2. peter rabbit _____
3. winnie-the-pooh _____
4. tony the tiger _____
5. templeton _____

Name/Date _____

Important Words 8

Write an example for each item list-ed. Capitalize all important words.

1. A political party _____
2. A religious group _____
3. A club _____
4. A school _____
5. A college _____

Name/Date _____

Important Words 9

Capitalize the important words in these movie ti-tles. When typing, use italics for movie titles. When writing, underline.

1. *the phantom of the opera* _____

   _____
2. *the wizard of oz* _____

   _____
3. *journey to the center of the earth* _____

   _____

Name/Date _____

Important Words 10

Capitalize the important words in these book titles. When typing, use italics for book titles. When writing, underline.

1. *cloudy with a chance of meatballs* _____

   _____
2. *the monster at the end of this book* _____

   _____
3. *harry potter and the deathly hallows* _____

   _____

Capitalization Warm-ups: Important Words

Name/Date _____

_____

Important Words 11

Underline the important words that should be capitalized in these nicknames of cities and states.

1. Illinois, the land of lincoln
2. Chicago, the windy city
3. Detroit, motor capital of the world
4. New York City, the big apple
5. Los Angeles, city of angels
6. Alaska, land of the midnight sun
7. Texas, the lone-star state
8. Missouri, the show-me state
9. Philadelphia, the city of brotherly love
10. New Jersey, the garden state

Name/Date _____

Important Words 12

Circle the 18 capitalization errors in this paragraph.

soylent green was a 1973 science-fiction movie starring charlton heston, edward g. robinson, leigh taylor-young, and chuck connors. It is loosely based on the 1966 science-fiction novella about overpopulation written by harry harrison, *make room! make room!*

Name/Date _____

Important Words 13

Capitalize the important words in addresses, including the two-letter abbreviations for states.
1. 1600 pennsylvania ave. _____
2. washington, d.c. _____
3. the field museum _____
4. lakeshore drive _____
5. chicago, il _____

Name/Date _____

Important Words 14

Should the underlined words be capitalized? Circle yes or no.

1. Yes No   Would you rather visit <u>mercury</u> or <u>mars</u>?
2. Yes No   The doctor's <u>office</u> is on a busy <u>street</u>.
3. Yes No   Angie moved to <u>san</u> <u>Francisco</u> in <u>july</u>.
4. Yes No   Many <u>states</u> charge to use the <u>highways</u>.
5 Yes No   <u>mount</u> <u>vesuvius</u> erupted in 79 A.D.

Name/Date _____

Important Words 15

Write an example for each item. Use proper capitalization.

1. a business _____
2. a computer program _____
3. a famous document _____
4. a major war _____
5. a major battle _____

Capitalization Warm-ups: Important Words

Name/Date _____

Important Words 16

Write an example for each item.
Capitalize the important words.

1. continents   _____
2. musical groups   _____
3. historical period _____
4. dramatic plays   _____
5. paintings   _____

Name/Date _____

Important Words 17

Capitalize the important words in nicknames.
Example: Randy Johnson, "the Big Unit"

1. Joe Namath, "broadway joe"
   _____
2. Joe Louis, "the brown bomber"
   _____
3. Benny Goodman, "the king of swing"
   _____
4. Babe Ruth, "the sultan of swat"
   _____

Name/Date _____

Important Words 18

Write an example for each item.
Use capitalization.

1. a national park _____
2. a monument   _____
3. a planet or star _____
4. a galaxy   _____

Name/Date _____

Important Words 19

Capitalize words like *mother* and titles like *doctor* only when they are part of a name. Underline the words that need to be capitalized.

1. Old mother Hubbard   2. judge Judy
3. office of the mayor   4. my vet's office
5. Dear aunt Sally   6. Jim, my uncle
7. president Bill Clinton 8. grandpa jones

Name/Date _____

Important Words 20

Capitalize direction words when they are parts of the country, part of any address, or part of the name of something. Rewrite the underlined words if the capitalization is incorrect.

1. the <u>northwest</u> Passage _____   2. 23 <u>south</u> Avenue _____
3. <u>southern</u> hospitality _____   4. <u>north</u> of the border _____
5. <u>east</u> St. Louis _____   6. the wild <u>west</u> _____
7. <u>southeast</u> of Miami _____   8. the <u>northern</u> lights _____

Capitalization Warm-ups:
Capitalization Review

Name/Date _____

Capitalization Review 1

1. T F Capitalize every word in the title of a book.
2. T F Always capitalize the words *mother* and *aunt*.
3. T F Never capitalize the word *the*.
4. T F Words like *in, an, on, to,* and *up* are important words and should always be capitalized.
5. T F Always capitalize the names of cities and states.

Name/Date _____

Capitalization Review 2

Mark the capitalization corrections needed.

1. mel blanc, the man who made the voice of bugs bunny famous, had an Allergy to carrots.
2. france presented the statue of Liberty to the united States in 1886. She weighs 225 tons. The Statue became a Symbol of Freedom for immigrants to the United States.

Name/Date _____

Capitalization Review 3

On your own paper, rewrite the paragraph with corrections.

   The words *september, october, november,* and *december* come from the latin words for Seven, Eight, Nine, and Ten. march (named for mars, the roman god of War) was the first month in the old roman calendar, so september was the seventh month, october the eighth, etc.

Name/Date _____

Capitalization Review 4

Mark the capitalization corrections needed.

   The Ancient greeks held athletic competitions every Four years, beginning about 776 B.C., to honor the god zeus, who they believed lived on mount olympus. Only Men competed in the original Greek olympic games. Women weren't even allowed to attend and could be executed for watching.

Name/Date _____

_____

Capitalization Review 5

Circle 10 words that name types of things that should be capitalized. Then write the words on the lines below.

```
S C H O O L S P
E P S E A S L E
G T S K K A S O
E T E D N E C P
L S E E T E O L
L E T A A E C E
O S T N M A P S
C S S S X S A B
```

1. _____
2. _____
3. _____
4. _____
5. _____
6. _____
7. _____
8. _____
9. _____
10. _____

Capitalization Warm-ups: Capitalization Review

Name/Date _____

_____

Capitalization Review 6

Circle 12 words that name types of things that should be capitalized. Then write the words on the lines below.

```
E  S  E  S  E  I  V  O  M
B  R  K  E  E  E  S  S  O
E  A  S  R  E  R  E  H  U
E  W  T  R  A  S  E  T  N
S  E  E  T  E  P  E  N  T
B  E  S  I  L  V  E  O  A
U  E  T  E  E  E  I  M  I
L  I  B  O  O  K  S  R  N
C  O  U  N  T  R  I  E  S
```

1. _____
2. _____
3. _____
4. _____
5. _____
6. _____
7. _____
8. _____
9. _____
10. _____
11. _____
12. _____

Name/Date _____

Capitalization Review 7

Circle the capitalization errors.

1. minnesota is known as "the land of 10,000 lakes."
2. There are really more than 10,000 Lakes in minnesota.
3. Mount saint helens, an active Volcano in the cascade mountains of southwestern washington, erupted on may 18, 1980.

Name/Date _____

Capitalization Review 8

On another sheet of paper, write a short thank-you letter to a friend or relative. Include your return address, a greeting, closing, and at least four sentences.

Name/Date _____

Capitalization Review 9

Use correct capitalization to write examples of each item.

1. a school   _____
2. a city you'd like to visit _____
3. a month   _____
4. a country   _____
5. a cartoon character _____

Name/Date _____

Capitalization Review 10

Mark the capitalization corrections needed.

The pittsburgh pirates were called the innocents until 1891, when the team signed second baseman lou bierbauer away from the philadelphia athletics. Philly fans weren't at all happy about this and dubbed his new club the pirates because they "pirated" their star player.

Capitalization & Punctuation Review

Capitalization & Punctuation Review 1

Correct the errors in the entry.

annie oakley broke every sharpshooting record in 1922 at the pinehurst gun club in north carolina by hitting 98 out of 100 targets. She could shoot a dime in midair and a cigarette from the lips of her Husband from 90 feet away

Capitalization & Punctuation Review 2

Correct the errors in the entry.

carry nation founder of the womens christian temperance union, preached against the evils of liquor. Waving a hatchet, she marched into saloons and smashed bottles She was often arrested for destroying property. She made public speeches and sold souvenir hatchets to help pay her court costs and fines.

Capitalization & Punctuation Review 3

Correct the errors in the entry. Write a headline for the news item using six words or less.

fannie farmer published america's first Cookbook, *the Boston cooking-School Cook Book* in 1896. She Then opened her famous cooking school in 1902. She wanted to make cooking a more Scientific process. Many women used recipes that called for a "pinch" of salt a "handful" of flour and a "dash" of cinnamon. She adopted standard measurements for cooking and became known as the "mother of level measurement."

THE ORIGINAL
FANNIE FARMER
1896
COOK BOOK
THE BOSTON
COOKING SCHOOL

Capitalization & Punctuation Review 4

All capitalization and punctuation has been removed from these song titles. Rewrite them correctly on another sheet of paper.

1. row row row your boat
2. how much is that doggie in the window
3. ive been working on the railroad
4. theres a hole in the bucket
5. the bear went over the mountain

Capitalization & Punctuation Review 5

All capitalization and punctuation has been removed from these literary titles. Rewrite them correctly on your own paper.

1. the emperors new clothes
2. jack and the beanstalk
3. a tale of peter rabbit
4. how the camel got his hump
5. the wolf in sheeps clothing

Capitalization & Punctuation Review

Capitalization & Punctuation Review 6

All punctuation and capitalization has been removed from these six proverbs. Rewrite them correctly on another sheet of paper.

1. dont cry over spilt milk
2. it never rains but it pours
3. rome wasnt built in a day
4. when in rome do as the romans do
5. curiosity killed the cat
6. the early bird catches the worm

Capitalization & Punctuation Review 7

All punctuation and capitalization has been removed from these six proverbs. Rewrite them correctly on another sheet of paper.

1. look before you leap
2. necessity is the mother of invention
3. beggars shouldnt be choosers
4. a rolling stone gathers no moss
5. all that glitters is not gold
6. a watched pot never boils

Capitalization & Punctuation Review 8

All punctuation and capitalization has been removed from these five proverbs. Rewrite them correctly on another sheet of paper.

1. a bird in the hand is worth two in the bush
2. dont change horses in the middle of a stream
3. dont cross the bridge until you get to it
4. you cant keep trouble from coming but you neednt give it a chair to sit on
5. you can lead students to knowledge but you cant make them think

Capitalization & Punctuation Review 9

All punctuation and capitalization has been removed from these six proverbs. Rewrite them correctly on another sheet of paper.

1. never look a gift horse in the mouth
2. when the cats away the mice will play
3. too many cooks spoil the broth
4. idle hands are the devils workshop
5. where the stall is clean there is no ox
6. you cant have your cake and eat it too

Capitalization & Punctuation Review 10

All punctuation and capitalization has been removed from these six proverbs. Rewrite them correctly on another sheet of paper.

1. beware of the wolf in sheeps clothing
2. dont kill the goose that lays the golden egg
3. you can lead a horse to water but you cant make it drink
4. you cant make a silk purse out of a sows ear
5. dont count your chickens until theyre hatched
6. laugh and the world laughs with you cry and you cry alone

Capitalization and Punctuation Proofreading

Name/Date _____

Proofreading 1

Correct the 10 capitalization and punctuation errors in the paragraph.

Todays submarine's are large compared to the one designed by david bush-nell during the revolutionary war. Called the *Turtle* it measured only seven and a half feet long and six feet wide. basically egg-shaped the *turtle* was constructed of oak and banded with iron. Riding in it must have seemed like being underwater in a barrel.

Name/Date _____

Proofreading 2

Correct the 9 capitalization and punctuation errors in the paragraph.

The *Turtle* could dive move underwater, and surface The Colonists planned to use it against british ships blocking new york harbor in 1776. In addition to being very small the *Turtle* had other problems. To move it under water, the Operator had to vigorously crank a hand-turned propeller.

Name/Date _____

Proofreading 3

Correct the 10 capitalization and punctuation errors in the paragraph.

air supply on the *turtle* was also a problem because it had none. The operator had to bring it to the Surface every 30 Minutes, or suffocate To descend the operator opened a valve to admit Seawater into a ballast tank. To ascend he emptied the tank with a Hand Pump.

Name/Date _____

Proofreading 4

Correct the 8 capitalization and punctuation errors in the paragraph.

The Submarine carried a gunpowder bomb with a time fuse. the *Turtle's* mission was to approach an enemy Ship. The operator planned to Attach the bomb to the ship's Hull using a screw device operated from within the Craft. Once the bomb was attached the *Turtle* needed to Escape before the bomb exploded.

Name/Date _____

Proofreading 5

Correct the 10 capitalization and punctuation errors in the paragraph.

sergeant ezra lee of the continental army made the one and only attempt to use the *Turtle* in battle. Lee floated the *Turtle* against the hull of the british flagship, the HMS *eagle* but could not attach the bomb because the ship hull was Copper-plated. Lee and the *Turtle* escaped but that was the end of the war for the *Turtle*.

Capitalization and Punctuation Proofreading

Name/Date _____

Proofreading 6

Correct the 12 capitalization and punctuation errors in the paragraph.
Note: *Tasmanian devil* is the correct form of capitalization for this animal.

What animal shrieks screams snorts growls and snarls; smells worse than a skunk; and eats carrion Early european explorers to australia named it the Tasmanian devil. These noisy, stinky animals live only in the forests and brush on the island of tasmania. The largest carnivorous Marsupial Tasmanian devils were once plentiful. However they are now protected due to their decreasing numbers

---

Name/Date _____

Proofreading 7

Correct the 8 errors in the paragraph.

Tasmanian devils weigh between 9 and 26 pounds They have large heads and teeth short stocky bodies and hairy tails Their blackish or brownish fur has white patches on the chest neck and rump. When excited the tasmanian devils pale pink ears turn deep red-purple. They are 20 to 31 inches long, with 9- to 12-inch tails. Males are larger than Females.

Name/Date _____

Proofreading 8

Correct the 6 errors in the paragraph.

These nocturnal Mammals hide in burrows hollow logs, or dense brush during the day. Tasmanian devil's live about eight years in the wild. Female's give birth to three or four tiny, blind young who stay in their mother's backwards-facing pouch for about four months The females pouch faces backwards to keep dirt out when the mother burrows.

Name/Date _____

Proofreading 9

Correct the 9 errors in the paragraph.

Young devils can climb trees but this becomes harder as they grow larger Tasmanian Devils are mostly solitary animals and do not form packs Although they have powerful, bone-crunching jaws, they are poor hunters They mainly eat dead or dying animals including the bones fur and Feathers.

Name/Date _____

Proofreading 10

Correct the errors in the paragraph.

Although Tasmanian devils were the inspiration for the cartoon character, Taz, there is only a slight resemblance between Taz and the real animals. Both have prominent canines, a large head, and short legs, but only Taz walks upright. Both Taz and the Tasmanian devils are noisy and have a voracious appetite.

Capitalization and Punctuation Proofreading

Name/Date _____

Proofreading 11

Correct the 8 errors in the paragraph.

In 1847 San francisco was a sleepy village of 800 on the pacific Coast Then gold was discovered nearby. San Francisco quickly grew to 15,000 by 1849 the population reached 25,000 by 1850. By 1856 san Francisco had more than 50,000 citizens and was the largest and most important city in the west.

Name/Date _____

Proofreading 12

Correct the 7 errors in the paragraph.

Ships carrying merchandise supplies and miners' to california usually landed in san francisco. Abandoned ships clogged the harbor, deserted by their crews who ran off to hunt for gold. Material from some ships was scavenged for building. Many of the ships' simply rotted.

Name/Date _____

Proofreading 13

Correct the 8 capitalization and punctuation errors in the paragraph.

When cities grow quickly, they tend to be crowded dirty and poorly planned. San Francisco was no exception. From a field of Tents and shacks, a town of houses and businesses grew almost overnight. Most streets were unpaved and few had sidewalks? When it rained mud and potholes made some streets impassible. So many buildings crowded closely together presented severe fire hazards A terrible fire broke out in May, 1851. In ten hours it destroyed 2,000 homes and much of the business district.

Name/Date _____

Proofreading 14

Correct the 7 errors in the paragraph.

Gradually new brick building's replaced the wooden ones! Labor was scare. Wages we're high but so was the Cost of living. The price of houses Skyrocketed to $75,000. Almost anyone willing to work could find a way to make money in San Francisco at that time without ever going to the gold mines

Name/Date _____

Proofreading 15

Correct the 5 errors in the paragraph.

The price of food supplies and services increased as much as 1,000%. rats infested the city. cats sold for $16 each. robberies were common. Most men carried weapons for protection, especially after dark on the unlit streets.

Answer Keys

Periods, Question Marks, & Exclamation Points 1 (p. 2)
1. How many chickens crossed the road?
2. Look out for that hole!
3. Does anyone know where the chickens went?
4. Come quickly!
5. Please put the feathers in the blue bag.
6. Someone should fill in that hole.

Periods, Question Marks, & Exclamation Points 2 (p. 2)
Answers will vary.

Periods, Question Marks, & Exclamation Points 3 (p. 2)
Answers will vary.

Periods, Question Marks, & Exclamation Points 4 (p. 2)
1. Nicole has a brother.
2. Jon will be ready by noon. or I think Jon will be ready by noon.
3. Tammy can win the race.

Periods, Question Marks, & Exclamation Points 5 (p. 2)
Answers will vary.

Periods, Question Marks, & Exclamation Points 6 (p. 3)
1. St.   2. Ave.   3. Mr.   4. Sr.
5. St.   6. in.   7. Jr.   8. Mt.

Periods, Question Marks, & Exclamation Points 7 (p. 3)
1. J. R. R. Tolkien   2. M. T. Lincoln
3. Mr. P. T. Barnum   4. Mrs. J. C. Parks
5. Dr. M. L. King, Jr.

Periods, Question Marks, & Exclamation Points 8 (p. 3)
1. True   2. False   3. True
4. False   5. False   6. True

Periods, Question Marks, & Exclamation Points 9 (p. 3)
1. Yes   2. No   3. No   4. No
5. Yes

Periods, Question Marks, & Exclamation Points 10 (p. 3)
Oh! Look at the shooting stars! Do you think one will land nearby? Have you ever seen so many shooting stars in one night? What a wonderful experience! I wonder if I will ever see a sight like this again? Dr Young, the astronomer, said this is a very rare event.

Commas 1 (p. 4)
1. Boise, Idaho   2. Paris, France
3. Taos, New Mexico   4. Moscow, Russia
5. Perth, Australia

Commas 2 (p. 4)
Answers will vary.

Commas 3 (p. 4)
1. How do oats, peas, beans, and barley grow?
2. Please pick up bread, milk, potatoes, carrots, and apples at the store.
3. Would you like macaroni and cheese or a bacon, lettuce, and tomato sandwich for lunch?
4. Do you prefer baseball, football, golf, hockey, or tennis?

Commas 4 (p. 4)
Answers will vary.

Commas 5 (p. 4)
1. July 4, 1776   2. February 1732
3. April 1885   4. September 1359
5. April 1, 1963   6. August 31, 1996
7. January 1, 2000   8. December 15, 1948

Commas 6 (p. 5)
1. "It is better to deserve honors," wrote Mark Twain, "and not have them than to have them and not to deserve them."
2. "Let us so live that when we come to die even the undertaker will be sorry," he said.
3. "My mother had a great deal of trouble with me," Twain admitted, "but I think she enjoyed it."
4. "Never put off until tomorrow what you can do the day after tomorrow," wrote Twain.
5. He also wrote, "It is better to keep your mouth closed and let people think you are a fool than to open it and remove all doubt."

Commas 7 (p. 5)
Answers will vary.

Commas 8 (p. 5)
1. Abby, the girl with the red scarf, left.
2. Tell Glen, who has freckles, that Abby left.
3. Abby, the girl who left, is Glen's cousin.
4. Glen, the quarterback, broke his ankle.
5. Abby, Glen's cousin, is going to the game.

Commas 9 (p. 5)
Answers will vary.

Commas 10 (p. 5)
1. Since you left, the phone rang nine times.
2. When we cook, the neighbors complain about the garlic smell.
3. Before you leave, the dog should be fed.
4. If Grandma bakes, her grandchildren will be delighted.
5. When it rains, cats and dogs get wet.

Commas 11 (p. 6)
Answers will vary.

Commas 12 (p. 6)
1. Abby, your mother called.
2. Your mother called, Abby
3. Glen, tell Abby her mother called.
4. Did you listen, Abby, to what Glen said?
5. I can't find Abby, Glen.

Commas 13 (p. 6)
Answers will vary.

Commas 14 (p. 6)
Dear Aunt Sally,

   Thank you for offering to bring dip, chips, and veggies for the cookout. Our neighbors, the Falks, have a dog. When we barbecue, the dog barks. Do you think I should buy dog treats? Then while we eat, the dog might be quiet for a while.

                              Your niece,
                              Sara

Commas 15 (p. 6)
1. Yes, we plan to meet Bret tomorrow after the game.
2. I wanted to stay for the postgame party, but Bret said no.
3. No, I don't know if Bret said yes or no to the contract.
4. Bret, did you decide to say yes to the contract?
5. "Yes, We Have No Bananas" is the name of an old song.

Commas 16 (p. 7)
1. When Abraham Lincoln was a lawyer, he carried important papers in his top hat.
2. Before he became president, Ulysses S. Grant was arrested twice for speeding.
3. For riding his horse too fast, he was fined $5.
4. George Washington, Thomas Jefferson, and John Adams enjoyed collecting and playing marbles, even as adults.

Commas 17 (p. 7)
1. John Quincy Adams, sixth president of the United States, planted mulberry trees on the White House lawn.
2. His wife, Louisa, spun silk from silkworms.
3. To relax, Adams liked to go for walks, play pool, and swim in the Potomac River.
4. Born in a log cabin, Millard Fillmore didn't attend school until he was 19 years old.

Commas 18 (p. 7)
   On December 17, 1903, Orville and Wilbur Wright made the first successful flight in a heavier-than-air machine. Their airplane didn't fly very far (only about 120 feet), very fast (only 30 mph), very high (only a few feet off the ground), or very long (only 12 seconds), but it did fly.

Commas 19 (p. 7)
   In 1938, Douglas Corrigan, an unemployed airplane mechanic, left Brooklyn, New York, to fly to Los Angeles, California. When he landed 28 hours and 13 minutes later, he found himself in Dublin, Ireland. Because he claimed he had accidentally followed the wrong end of the compass needle, he received the nickname "Wrong Way" Corrigan.

Commas 20 (p. 7)
1. D   2. G   3. E   4. H   5. C   6. A
7. F   8. B

Commas 21 (p. 8)
1. Yes   2. No   3. Yes   4. No
5. No   6. No

Commas 22 (p. 8)
Answers will vary.

Commas 23 (p. 8)
Answers will vary.

Commas 24 (p. 8)
Answers will vary.

Commas 25 (p. 8)
Answers will vary.

Apostrophes to Show Possession 1 (p. 9)
1. the hens' eggs   2. the families' homes
3. the women's gardens   4. the bees' honey
5. the forests' trees   6. the teachers' desks

Apostrophes to Show Possession 2 (p. 9)
1. the child's song   2. the deer's antlers
3. the mouse's tail   4. the rose's scent
5. Italy's capital

Apostrophes to Show Possession 3 (p. 9)
1. the buses' wheels   2. the children's laughter
3. the factories' sounds 4. the ladies' gardens
5. the wolves' howls

Apostrophes to Show Possession 4 (p. 9)
1. the tiger's tales   2. the bear's growls
3. the city's lights   4. the man's children
5. the horse's shoes   6. Maine's cities

Apostrophes to Show Possession 5 (p. 9)
1. the sharks' teeth   2. the foxes' feet
3. the bushes' berries   4. the mice's squeals
5. the elves' scarves

Apostrophes to Show Possession 6 (p. 10)
Answers will vary.

Apostrophes to Show Possession 7 (p. 10)
Answers will vary.

Apostrophes to Show Possession 8 (p. 10)
Singular possessive nouns will vary.
1. leaves   2. feet   3. men
4. cherries   5. teeth   6. animals

Apostrophes to Show Possession 9 (p. 10)
Plural possessive nouns will vary.
1. flowers   2. horses   3. firemen
4. geese   5. fish or fishes

Apostrophes to Show Possession 10 (p. 10)
Singular nouns will vary.
1. groups'   2. aunts'   3. monkeys'
4. people's   5. puppies'   6. buddies'

Apostrophes to Show Possession 11 (p. 11)
Plural nouns will vary.
1. spies'   2. moose's   3. oxen's
4. pianos'   5. tomatoes' 6. mosquitoes'

Apostrophes to Show Possession 12 (p. 11)
1. Yes   2. No   3. No   4. Yes
5. No   6. No

Apostrophes to Show Possession 13 (p. 11)
1. its   2. Sue's   3. daisy's or daisies'
4. your   5. grandmother's   6. grandfathers

Apostrophes to Show Possession 14 (p. 11)
Answers will vary.

Apostrophes to Show Possession 15 (p. 11)
1. "A countryman between two <u>lawyers</u> is like a fish between two <u>cats</u>."
2. "<u>Humans</u> are not proud of their <u>ancestors</u>, and rarely invite them round to dinner."
3. "Do not worry about your <u>difficulties</u> in <u>Mathematics</u>. I can assure you mine are still greater."
4. "A <u>nation's</u> treasure is in its <u>scholars</u>."

Apostrophes With Contractions 1 (p. 12)
1. I'm   2. you're   3. he's   4. she'll
5. isn't   6. it'd   7. they'd   8. we've

Apostrophes With Contractions 2 (p. 12)
1. aren't   2. won't   3. they'll   4. could've
5. we're   6. where's 7. couldn't   8. how's

Apostrophes With Contractions 3 (p. 12)
1. can't   2. Don't   3. Birds
4. We're   5. He's   6. It's

Apostrophes With Contractions 4 (p. 12)
1. he'd   2. she'd   3. I'll   4. they're
5. it's   6. we're   7. you've   8. mustn't

Apostrophes With Contractions 5 (p. 12)
1. isn't   2. won't   3. We're   4. teacher's

Apostrophes With Contractions 6 (p. 13)
1. don't   2. I'd   3. doesn't 4. she's
5. didn't   6. we'd   7. he'd   8. hasn't

Apostrophes With Contractions 7 (p. 13)
1. they'd   2. he'll   3. can't   4. how'd
5. hadn't   6. haven't 7. he's   8. how'd

Apostrophes With Contractions 8 (p. 13)
1. won't   2. She's   3. That's   4. didn't

Apostrophes With Contractions 9 (p. 13)
1. I've   2. how's   3. I'd   4. must've
5. mightn't 6. should've 7. we've   8. weren't

Apostrophes With Contractions 10 (p. 13)
1. doesn't   2. Don't; It's   3. I'm   4. we'd

Apostrophes With Contractions 11 (p. 14)
1. it'd   2. it'll   3. might've   4. she'd
5. that'll   6. we'll   7. they'd   8. who'll

Apostrophes With Contractions 12 (p. 14)
1. it's   2. she's   3. shouldn't   4. that'd
5. they've   6. wasn't   7. we'd   8. who's

Apostrophes With Contractions 13 (p. 14)
1. They're   2. She'll   3. wouldn't
4. That's   5. You're

Apostrophes With Contractions 14 (p. 14)
1. that's   2. when'll   3. we'll   4. who'd
5. would've   6. you've   7. wouldn't   8. you'd

Apostrophes With Contractions 15 (p. 14)
1. when's   2. you'll   3. we'd   4. what're
5. what'll   6. where'll   7. what's   8. who's

Apostrophe Review 1 (p. 15)
1. It's; your   2. its   3. your
4. Whose   5. Who's

Apostrophe Review 2 (p. 15)
1. Who's   2. whose   3. They're
4. there   5. their

Apostrophe Review 3 (p. 15)
1. theirs   2. There's   3. There's
4. Who's   5. You're

Apostrophe Review 4 (p. 15)
1. boys'   2. Greece's   3. *Hitchhiker's*
4. frog's   5. Jackson's

Apostrophe Review 5 (p. 15)
1. giraffe's   Long enough to reach the ground.
2. dinosaurs   Baby dinosaurs.
3. animals   Mice, because they squeak.
4. ant's   Whatever it puts in its mouth.
5. Ranger's   The

Quotation Marks 1 (p. 16)
Answers will vary.

Quotation Marks 2 (p. 16)
Answers will vary.

Quotation Marks 3 (p. 16)
1. "Ox Cart Drag Racing"
2. "Football Stars from the Past"
3. "7 Ways to Become a Millionaire"
4. "The Best Artichoke Recipes"
5. "Dog with College Degree Called to Court"

Quotation Marks 4 (p. 16)
Answers will vary.

Quotation Marks 5 (p. 16)
Answers will vary.

Quotation Marks 6 (p. 17)
1. "O Captain! My Captain!" is a famous poem about Abraham Lincoln by Walt Whitman.
2. The television show "Gunsmoke" was on the air for 20 years.
3. Many people continue to enjoy watching reruns of "Star Trek."
4. Did you read the article "Girl Calls 911: Grandpa Cheats at Cards" today?

Quotation Marks 7 (p. 17)
1. Sara shouted, "Look out!"
2. "Are we there yet?" Tina asked.
3. Tammy answered, "We'll be there soon."
4. "But when?" Tina whined.
5. "Where did you come from?" Troy asked

Quotation Marks 8 (p. 17)
1. "Suddenly," said Caesar, "I understand what you mean."
2. "I may not have gone where I intended to go," wrote Douglas Adams, "but I think I have ended up where I needed to be."
3. "It is a mistake," the author of *The Hitchhiker's Guide to the Galaxy* wrote, "to think you can solve any major problems just with potatoes."
4. "Please buy some eggs," George told his son, "and also a gallon of milk."

Quotation Marks 9 (p. 17)
Answers will vary.

Quotation Marks 10 (p. 17)
Answers will vary.

Colons & Semicolons 1 (p. 18)
1. Brian thought she was kind; I thought she was grouchy.
2. "I came; I saw; I conquered," wrote Julius Caesar.
3. Jessica wrote short stores; she also wrote poetry.

4. Pam needed a new coat; her old one was too small.
5. The blizzard was bad; the planes could not land.

Colons & Semicolons 2 (p. 18)
Dear Mayor:

After attending the 7:00 meeting last evening, I had three concerns: the number of snowplows available, the training of personnel, and the plowing schedule for the school parking lots.

Colons & Semicolons 3 (p. 18)
Dear Mr. Jones:

I will arrive at 6:30 today to pick up the six items for my office we discussed: the new computer, printer, monitor, scanner, telephone, and desk.
Sincerely,
Matt Pyatt

Colons & Semicolons 4 (p. 18)
Dear Brenda,

Please do these chores when you get home at 3:00: clean your room, start the laundry, and put the roast in the oven. I will see you at 5:45; your father will be home at 6:00.
Mom

Colons & Semicolons 5 (p. 18)
Answers will vary.

Punctuation Review 1 (p. 19)
Answers will vary.

Punctuation Review 2 (p. 19)
1. period; question mark; exclamation point
2. question mark   3. exclamation point
4. period   5. period

Punctuation Review 3 (p. 19)
1. Harry Potter, the boy who lived, is a fictional character.
2. While Doris ate, the mice waited for crumbs.
3. After Jen finished sweeping, the wind blew the dirt back.
4. Until 1958, the Dodgers played in Brooklyn, New York.
5. Paul, please wash, dry, and put away the dishes.

Punctuation Review 4 (p. 19)
In 1885, Gottlieb Daimler, a German inventor, built the first motorcycle by attaching a small gasoline engine to a wooden bicycle frame. The wooden wheels came from a horse-drawn carriage; the seat was a leather horse's saddle. Early motorcycles had pedals like bikes. The engines weren't strong enough to go up hills, so riders had to pedal.

Punctuation Review 5 (p. 19)
The engines on early motorcycles weren't very reliable. Unfortunately, they often broke down. Riders carried gasoline with them because there were no gas stations. Fortunately, if the engine didn't work or the motorcycle ran out of gas, the rider could always keep pedaling. Can you imagine a group of Harley riders pedaling down the highway today?

Punctuation Review 6 (p. 20)
1. No; Henry Wadsworth Longfellow's poem, "Paul Revere's Ride," was very popular in the 1860s.
2. No; Longfellow wrote about a real event, but he changed the facts a bit.
3. Yes
4. Yes
5. No; On the night of April 18, 1775, Paul Revere left Boston.
6. No; Revere rode to Lexington to warn Samuel Adams and John Hancock that British soldiers planned to arrest them.

Punctuation Review 7 (p. 20)
1. Yes
2. No; On his way to Lexington, he stopped at houses to deliver a warning.
3. No; William Dawes also set out to deliver the same warnings, but he took a different route.

Punctuation Review 8 (p. 20)
1. Yes
2. No; About midnight, he gave Adams and Hancock the message; they had time to escape.
3. Yes

Punctuation Review 9 (p. 20)
1. No; On the way, Dr. Samuel Prescott joined them.
2. Yes
3. No; Dawes and Prescott escaped, but Dawes fell off his horse.
4. Yes

Punctuation Review 10 (p. 20)
1. No; The British took away Paul Revere's horse.
2. Yes
3. No; Prescott reached Concord.
4. No; Prescott's early warning helped the patriots win the first battle of the Revolutionary War.

Punctuation Review 11 (p. 21)
Answers will vary.

Punctuation Review 12 (p. 21)
Answers will vary.

Punctuation Review 13 (p. 21)
Answers will vary.

Punctuation Review 14 (p. 21)
Answers will vary.

Punctuation Review 15 (p. 21)
    Buffalo Bill Cody had little formal education. When he wrote his life story, the publisher complained about Cody's punctuation and capitalization. "Life is too short to make big letters where small ones will do," replied Cody. "And as for punctuation, if my readers don't know enough to take their breath without those little marks, they'll have to lose it, that's all."

Punctuation Review 16 (p. 22)
1. punctuation
2. quotation marks
3. comma
4. question marks
5. exclamation point
6. colons
7. semicolons
8. apostrophes
9. period

Punctuation Review 17 (p. 22)
1. Yours truly,
2. Dear Angie,
3. May 1, 1902
4. 4:15 A.M.
5. Rome, Italy

Punctuation Review 18 (p. 22)
1. Pecos Bill, a cowboy, was a hero in many tall tales.
2. Sam, have you ever wanted to be a superhero?
3. What would be a good name for a superhero hamster, Herman?
4. Mighty Mouse, a cartoon character, always arrived in the nick of time.

Punctuation Review 19 (p. 22)
1. Spitting on your hands before picking up the bat is good luck.
2. A wad of gum stuck on a player's hat is good luck.
3. It is bad luck if a dog walks across the diamond.
4. Lending a bat to a fellow player brings bad luck.
5. Sleeping with your bat will help end a hitting slump.

Punctuation Review 20 (p. 22)
1. A rolling stone gathers no moss.
2. Every cloud has a silver lining.
3. A stitch in time saves nine.
4. A penny saved is a penny earned.
5. You can't teach an old dog new tricks.

Proper Nouns 1 (p. 23)
Answers will vary.

Proper Nouns 2 (p. 23)
Answers will vary.

Proper Nouns 3 (p. 23)
Answers will vary.

Proper Nouns 4 (p. 23)
Answers will vary.

Proper Nouns 5 (p. 23)
1. Sunday, March 15, we will travel to Mexico.
2. Thanksgiving is celebrated on the fourth Thursday in November.
3. For supper, Jason ordered a salad with French dressing, German chocolate cake, and Italian spaghetti.
4. Dolly Madison, Mary Todd Lincoln, Abigail Adams, and Martha Washington were famous first ladies.

Proper Nouns 6 (p. 24)
1. In 1656, Captain Kemble of Boston was sentenced to sit in the stocks for two hours because of improper behavior on a Sunday.
2. He had kissed his wife in public after returning from a three-year sea voyage!
3. A dog was convicted of killing a cat and sent to prison in 1925.
4. He died of old age after spending his last six years in a prison in Philadelphia.
5. In 1939, pinball machines were illegal in Atlanta, Georgia.
6. In 1660, Massachusetts outlawed the celebration of Christmas.
7. Offenders were fined five shillings.

Proper Nouns 7 (p. 24)
1. In Philadelphia, Pennsylvania, in 1912, 15 women lost their jobs at the Curtis Publishing Company for dancing at work.
2. In 1674, 30 men were arrested in Connecticut for wearing silk and having long hair.
3. In 1712, people who drove their wagons recklessly in Philadelphia were fined for speeding.

Proper Nouns 8 (p. 24)
1. Electricity was installed in the White House while Benjamin Harrison was president.
2. Harrison and his wife feared it; they refused to touch any of the switches.
3. Sometimes they left the lights on all night if servants weren't available to turn them off.
4. President Jackson had little formal education as a child.

Proper Nouns 9 (p. 24)
1. Honey discovered in the tombs of Egyptian pharaohs is still edible.
2. Egyptians believed that the creator god, Khnum, made each person on his potter's wheel.
3. The Greek historian Herodotus reported that when a family's pet cat died, Egyptians mourned the loss by shaving off their eyebrows.

Proper Nouns 10 (p. 24)
1. The ancient Egyptians had a taxation and legal system with a police force and courts.
2. One way to pay taxes was to send servants to work part of the year for the pharaoh.
3. Beating was the most common form of punishment for criminals and those who did not pay their taxes.

Proper Nouns 11–14 (p. 25)
Answers will vary.

Proper Nouns 15 (p. 15)
(George) (Samuelson) and (Frank) (Harbo) crossed the (Atlantic) (Ocean) in 1894. (They) left (New) (York) on (June) 6 and landed safely in (England) on (August) 1, 1894. (George) and (Frank) weren't the first to make the perilous (journey) across the (ocean), but they did it the hard way—in a (rowboat)!

Important Words 1 (p. 26)
1. King Henry of England
2. Emperor Julius Caesar
3. Queen Isabella of Spain
4. President Gerald R. Ford
5. Lawrence of Arabia

Important Words 2 (p. 26)
1. the Grand Canyon
2. the Golden Gate Bridge
3. St. Louis Gateway Arch
4. the Pyramids of Giza
5. Mount St. Helens

Important Words 3 (p. 26)
Answers will vary.

Important Words 4 (p. 26)
1. the Constitution
2. the Statue of Liberty
3. the Great Wall of China
4. the Taj Mahal
5. the Gettysburg Address

Important Words 5 (p. 26)
The statue of Zeus at Olympia was one of the seven wonders of the ancient world. This 40-foot-tall seated figure of Zeus, king of the Greek gods, was carved in the mid-5th century B.C. by Phidias. It was the central feature of the temple of Zeus at Olympia, home to the ancient Olympic Games in Greece.

Important Words 6 (p. 27)
1. In 1970, a 1.67 pound hailstone fell in Coffeyville, Texas.
2. An earthquake in Missouri on November 16, 1811, caused the Mississippi River to flow backwards.
3. George Washington had two ice-cream freezers at his home in Mount Vernon.
4. Mother Nature dumped 189 inches of snow on Mount Shasta, California, during a storm that lasted from February 13 to 19, 1959.

Important Words 7 (p. 27)
1. Bugs Bunny
2. Peter Rabbit
3. Winnie-the-Pooh
4. Tony the Tiger
5. Templeton

Important Words 8 (p. 27)
Answers will vary.

Important Words 9 (p. 27)
1. *The Phantom of the Opera*
2. *The Wizard of Oz*
3. *Journey to the Center of the Earth*

Important Words 10 (p. 27)
1. *Cloudy with a Chance of Meatballs*
2. *The Monster at the End of this Book*
3. *Harry Potter and the Deathly Hallows*

Important Words 11 (p. 28)
1. Illinois, the Land of Lincoln
2. Chicago, the Windy City
3. Detroit, Motor Capital of the World
4. New York, the Big Apple
5. Los Angeles, City of Angels
6. Alaska, Land of the Midnight Sun
7. Texas, the Lone-Star State
8. Missouri, the Show-Me State
9. Philadelphia, the City of Brotherly Love
10. New Jersey, the Garden State

Important Words 12 (p. 28)
Soylent Green was a 1973 science-fiction movie starring Charlton Heston, Edward G. Robinson, Leigh Taylor-Young, and Chuck Connors. It is loosely based on the 1966 science-fiction novella about overpopulation written by Harry Harrison, *Make Room! Make Room!*

Important Words 13 (p. 28)
1. 1600 Pennsylvania Ave.
2. Washington, D.C.
3. the Field Museum
4. Lakeshore Drive
5. Chicago, IL

Important Words 14 (p. 28)
1. Yes   2. No   3. Yes   4. No
5. Yes

Important Words 15 (p. 28)
Answers will vary.

Important Words 16 (p. 29)
Answers will vary.

Important Words 17 (p. 29)
1. "Broadway Joe"   2. "the Brown Bomber"
3. "the King of Swing"   4. "the Sultan of Swat"

Important Words 18 (p. 29)
Answers will vary.

Important Words 19 (p. 29)
1. Old Mother Hubbard   2. Judge Judy
3. office of the mayor   4. my vet's office
5. Dear Aunt Sally   6. Jim, my uncle
7. President Bill Clinton   8. Grandpa Jones

Important Words 20 (p. 29)
1. the Northwest Passage
2. 23 South Avenue
3. Southern hospitality
4. north of the border
5. East St. Louis
6. the wild West
7. southeast of Miami
8. the northern lights

Capitalization Review 1 (p. 30)
1. F   2. F   3. F   4. F   5. T

Capitalization Review 2 (p. 30)
1. Mel Blanc, the man who made the voice of Bugs Bunny famous, had an allergy to carrots.
2. France presented the Statue of Liberty to the United States in 1886. She weighs 225 tons. The statue became a symbol of freedom for immigrants to the United States.

Capitalization Review 3 (p. 30)
The words *September, October, November,* and *December* come from the Latin words for seven, eight, nine, and ten. March (named for Mars, the Roman god of war) was the first month in the old Roman calendar, so September was the seventh month, October the eighth, etc.

Capitalization Review 4 (p. 30)
The ancient Greeks held athletic competitions every four years, beginning about 776 B.C., to honor the god Zeus, who they believed lived on Mount Olympus. Only men competed in the original Greek Olympic Games. Women weren't even allowed to attend and could be executed for watching.

Capitalization Review 5 (p. 30)
Answers in any order:

colleges	lakes
oceans	people
planets	poems
schools	seas
states	teams

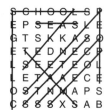

Capitalization Review 6 (p. 31)
Answers in any order:

battles	books
cities	clubs
countries	parks
mountains	movies
months	rivers
stars	wars

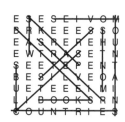

Capitalization Review 7 (p. 31)
1. Minnesota is known as "the Land of 10,000 Lakes."
2. There are really more than 10,000 lakes in Minnesota.
3. Mount Saint Helens, an active volcano in the Cascade Mountains of southwestern Washington, erupted on May 18, 1980.

Capitalization Review 8–9 (p. 31)
Answers will vary.

Capitalization Review 10 (p. 31)
The Pittsburgh Pirates were called the Innocents until 1891, when the team signed second baseman Lou Bierbauer away from the Philadelphia Athletics. Philly fans weren't at all happy about this and dubbed his new club the Pirates because they "pirated" their star player.

Capitalization & Punctuation Review 1 (p. 32)

Annie Oakley broke every sharpshooting record in 1922 at the Pinehurst Gun Club in North Carolina by hitting 98 out of 100 targets. She could shoot a dime in midair and a cigarette from the lips of her husband from 90 feet away.

Capitalization & Punctuation Review 2 (p. 32)

Carry Nation, founder of the Women's Christian Temperance Union, preached against the evils of liquor. Waving a hatchet, she marched into saloons and smashed bottles. She was often arrested for destroying property. She made public speeches and sold souvenir hatchets to help pay her court costs and fines.

Capitalization & Punctuation Review 3 (p. 32)

Headlines will vary.

Fannie Farmer published America's first cookbook, *The Boston Cooking-School Cook Book,* in 1896. She then opened her famous cooking school in 1902. She wanted to make cooking a more scientific process. Many women used recipes that called for a "pinch" of salt, a "handful" of flour, and a "dash" of cinnamon. She adopted standard measurements for cooking and became known as the "Mother of Level Measurement."

Capitalization & Punctuation Review 4 (p. 32)

1. "Row, Row, Row Your Boat"
2. "How Much is that Doggie in the Window?"
3. "I've Been Working on the Railroad"
4. "There's a Hole in the Bucket"
5. "The Bear Went Over the Mountain"

Capitalization & Punctuation Review 5 (p. 32)

1. "The Emperor's New Clothes"
2. "Jack and the Beanstalk"
3. "A Tale of Peter Rabbit"
4. "How the Camel Got His Hump"
5. "The Wolf in Sheep's Clothing"

Capitalization & Punctuation Review 6 (p. 33)

1. Don't cry over spilt milk.
2. It never rains, but it pours.
3. Rome wasn't built in a day.
4. When in Rome, do as the Romans do.
5. Curiosity killed the cat.
6. The early bird catches the worm.

Capitalization & Punctuation Review 7 (p. 33)

1. Look before you leap.
2. Necessity is the mother of invention.
3. Beggars shouldn't be choosers.
4. A rolling stone gathers no moss.
5. All that glitters is not gold.
6. A watched pot never boils.

Capitalization & Punctuation Review 8 (p. 33)

1. A bird in the hand is worth two in the bush.
2. Don't change horses in the middle of a stream.
3. Don't cross the bridge until you get to it.
4. You can't keep trouble from coming, but you needn't give it a chair to sit on.
5. You can lead students to knowledge, but you can't make them think.

Capitalization & Punctuation Review 9 (p. 33)

1. Never look a gift horse in the mouth.
2. When the cat's away, the mice will play.
3. Too many cooks spoil the broth.
4. Idle hands are the devil's workshop.
5. Where the stall is clean, there is no ox.
6. You can't have your cake and eat it too.

Capitalization & Punctuation Review 10 (p. 33)

1. Beware of the wolf in sheep's clothing.
2. Don't kill the goose that lays the golden egg.
3. You can lead a horse to water, but you can't make it drink.
4. You can't make a silk purse out of a sow's ear.
5. Don't count your chickens until they're hatched.
6. Laugh and the world laughs with you. Cry and you cry alone.

Proofreading 1 (p. 34)

Today's submarines are large compared to the one designed by David Bushnell during the Revolutionary War. Called the *Turtle,* it measured only seven and a half feet long and six feet wide. Basically egg-shaped, the *Turtle* was constructed of oak and banded with iron. Riding in it must have seemed like being underwater in a barrel.

Proofreading 2 (p. 34)

The *Turtle* could dive, move underwater, and surface. The colonists planned to use it against British ships blocking New York Harbor in 1776. In addition to being very small, the *Turtle* had other problems. To move it under water, the operator had to vigorously crank a hand-turned propeller.

Proofreading 3 (p. 34)

Air supply on the *Turtle* was also a problem because it had none. The operator had to bring it to the surface every 30 minutes, or suffocate. To descend, the operator opened a valve to admit seawater into a ballast tank. To ascend, he emptied the tank with a hand pump.

Proofreading 4 (p. 34)

The submarine carried a gunpowder bomb with a time fuse. The *Turtle's* mission was to approach an enemy ship. The operator planned to attach the bomb to the ship's hull using a screw device operated from within the craft. Once the bomb was attached, the *Turtle* needed to escape before the bomb exploded.

Proofreading 5 (p. 34)

Sergeant Ezra Lee of the Continental Army made the one and only attempt to use the *Turtle* in battle. Lee floated the *Turtle* against the hull of the British flagship, the HMS *Eagle,* but could not attach the bomb because the ship's hull was copper-plated. Lee and the *Turtle* escaped, but that was the end of the war for the *Turtle.*

Proofreading 6 (p. 35)

What animal shrieks, screams, snorts, growls, and snarls; smells worse than a skunk; and eats carrion? Early European explorers to Australia named it the Tasmanian devil. These noisy, stinky animals live only in the forests and brush on the island of Tasmania. The largest carnivorous marsupial, Tasmanian devils were once plentiful. However, they are now protected due to their decreasing numbers.

Proofreading 7 (p. 35)

Tasmanian devils weigh between 9 and 26 pounds. They have large heads and teeth, short stocky bodies, and hairy tails. Their blackish or brownish fur has white patches on the chest, neck, and rump. When excited, the Tasmanian devil's pale pink ears turn deep red-purple. They are 20 to 31 inches long, with 9- to 12-inch tails. Males are larger than females.

Proofreading 8 (p. 35)

These nocturnal mammals hide in burrows, hollow logs, or dense brush during the day. Tasmanian devils live about eight years in the wild. Females give birth to three or four tiny, blind young who stay in their mother's backwards-facing pouch for about four months. The female's pouch faces backwards to keep dirt out when the mother burrows.

Proofreading 9 (p. 35)

Young devils can climb trees, but this becomes more difficult as they grow larger. Tasmanian devils are mostly solitary animals and do not form packs. Although they have powerful, bone-crunching jaws, they are poor hunters. They mainly eat dead or dying animals, including the bones, fur, and feathers.

Proofreading 10 (p. 35)

There are no errors in this paragraph.

Proofreading 11 (p. 36)

In 1847, San Francisco was a sleepy village of 800 on the Pacific Coast. Then gold was discovered nearby. San Francisco quickly grew to 15,000 by 1849; the population reached 25,000 by 1850. By 1856, San Francisco had more than 50,000 citizens and was the largest and most important city in the West.

Proofreading 12 (p. 36)

Ships carrying merchandise, supplies, and miners to California usually landed in San Francisco. Abandoned ships clogged the harbor, deserted by their crews who ran off to hunt for gold. Material from some ships was scavenged for building. Many of the ships simply rotted.

Proofreading 13 (p. 36)

When cities grow quickly, they tend to be crowded, dirty, and poorly planned. San Francisco was no exception. From a field of tents and shacks, a town of houses and businesses grew almost overnight. Most streets were unpaved and few had sidewalks. When it rained, mud and potholes made some streets impassible. So many buildings crowded closely together presented severe fire hazards. A terrible fire broke out in May 1851. In ten hours, it destroyed 2,000 homes and much of the business district.

Proofreading 14 (p. 36)

Gradually new brick buildings replaced the wooden ones. Labor was scare. Wages were high, but so was the cost of living. The price of houses skyrocketed to $75,000. Almost anyone willing to work could find a way to make money in San Francisco at that time without ever going to the gold mines.

Proofreading 15 (p. 36)

The price of food, supplies, and services increased as much as 1,000%. Rats infested the city. Cats sold for $16 each. Robberies were common. Most men carried weapons for protection, especially after dark on the unlit streets.